The Christmas Angels

For my friend, Liz ~ C F

To my two little angels, Abigail and William
— you're my inspiration ~ G Y

Copyright © 2008 by Good Books, Intercourse, PA 17534
International Standard Book Number: 978-1-56148-637-3

Text copyright © Claire Freedman 2008
Illustrations copyright © Gail Yerrill 2008

Original edition published in English by Little Tiger Press,
an imprint of Magi Publications, London, England, 2008.
Printed in China

Library of Congress Cataloging-in-Publication Data available

The Christmas Angels

CLAIRE FREEDMAN

Illustrated by GAIL YERRILL

Good Books

Intercourse, PA 17534
800/762-7171
www.GoodBooks.com

Hush now, can you hear
the angels singing,
High up in the
frosty midnight air?
Voices ringing, singing
songs of Christmas,
Happiness for all
the world to share.

As we count the days

until it's Christmas,

Filling all our homes

with light and love,

Angels share these

special times of gladness,

Celebrating with us

high above.

As the snowflakes float like stars from heaven,

Angels touch them softly, one by one,

Giving each a gentle angel blessing,

Snowflakes sent with love for everyone.

When we gather 'round
to sing sweet carols,
Each of us with
happy heart aglow,
In the sky, the angels
all sing with us,
As on that first
Christmas long ago.

By our sides, our caring

guardian angels

Look out for us,

each and every day.

So, however far from

home we travel,

Loving angels help

us on our way.

When we help and care
for one another,
High above, the angels
see it too.
Every little act of
love and kindness,
Makes the gentle angels
smile at you.

As dusk falls, the angels fly above us,

Lighting all the stars up in the sky.

When you see a silver star shine brightly,

Then you know an angel is nearby.

Angels sing their songs

of treasured friendship,

Special moments,

sharing everything,

Songs about our

happy times together,

And the warmth that

loving friendships bring.

As the daylight fades

to gentle shadows,

And soft moonbeams

shimmer, silver-white,

Tender angels watch us

while we're sleeping,

Keeping us safe through

the moonlit night.

Hush now, can you hear the angels singing?

Sweetest songs of peace from heaven above,

Christmas songs of hope and joy and wonder,

Filling every happy heart with love.